It Happened to to Me

*Behind the Smile: The Hurts, The Pains, and
God's Hands of Protection*

Tina Jenkins-Wilson

ISBN 978-1-0980-8594-0 (paperback)
ISBN 978-1-0980-8595-7 (digital)

Christian Faith Publishing, Inc.
832 Park Avenue
Meadville, PA 16335
www.christianfaithpublishing.com

Printed in the United States of America

Foreword

Perhaps one of the biggest misconceptions about becoming a Christian is that once we become born again, nothing bad will ever happen to us. I believe that is often one of the worst forms of false advertisement presented to new believers. It's as if the church sometimes feels that in order to make Christianity appealing, it must paint a picture that once we accept Christ in all His perfection, our lives will be perfect, and we'll never again experience difficulties. Nothing is further from the truth! The Bible is clear about this when it says, "The righteous person faces many troubles, but the Lord comes to the rescue each time" (Ps. 34:19 NLT). In fact, if you search the word "trouble" in the Bible, there are so many scriptures that encourage believers not to give up when faced with challenges and trying circumstances. In other words, as believers, we *will* face difficulties at times, but the good news is that we never have to face them alone. God is always there walking through the fire with us! The prophet Isaiah said it this way, "When you go through deep waters, I will be with you. When you go through rivers of difficulty, you will not drown. When you walk through the fire of oppression, you will not be burned up; the flames will not consume you" (Isa. 43:2 NLT).

This realization that trouble is inevitable, even in the life of the believer, makes it imperative for us to learn how to overcome our circumstances instead of allowing them to overcome us. In this book, my sister (not by blood but might as well be) and BFF (best friends and family forever) takes us on a very personal and painful journey in how she learned the meaning of the word "overcome." At first glance, one might think Tina's life is and has always been perfect. She exudes beauty, success, strength, and prosperity. Her life reflects her relationship with God and tells of His goodness. When you see her, more often than not, she has a huge smile on her face, is laughing it up with her family and friends, enjoying life. She is certainly the life of the party even though she's usually not trying to be. Tina is one of those people who steps into a room, and everyone notices her. Her energy is magnetic, and it commands attention. But there is much more to her story than what meets the eye.

When I first met Tina over twenty years ago, there was an instant connection. Neither of us knew at the time that we'd become the best of friends, but our stories traveled similar paths. Both of us grew up in ministry families, and we both had fathers who were former NFL players. Our parents were friends before we were. Upon meeting her, I could sense that she was very selective in the company she kept. She wasn't the kind of person that just let everyone into her personal space. She was very observant and discerning when it came to the people who were around her. The reason that I could so easily detect these characteristics in her is because I was the same way. When you grow up as a minister's kid and with a father who is a former professional athlete like we both did, there is a certain spotlight that you live under. You quickly learn to recognize people who may have ulterior motives, which usually results in your inner circle being very small. You learn to choose your relationships wisely and carefully. Because I could relate to this part of Tina's personality, I wasn't intimidated by it at all. I think it was probably one of the things that caused us to both let our guards down because we had common ground.

Some people you encounter end up being good friends, and others end up being godsent. It was evident from the beginning that God connected me and Tina. Although she was obviously a strong, spiritually grounded, very confident person, I knew there was something fragile underneath that solid exterior. It was strange, but almost immediately, God revealed that to me about her. But I had no idea the extent of what she had been through. There's an old saying in the church that goes "I don't look like what I've been through." Tina certainly embodies this.

When we met, she was a devoted wife and mother of two young children, a successful entrepreneur, a faithful follower of Christ who was very active in her church, and one of the baddest ("bad" meaning great) cooks from whom I'd ever have the pleasure of sampling food! Did I mention her peach cobbler makes you want to slap your momma? The irony is that she's also one of the best fitness trainers and nutritionists in the business. So after you get fat from eating her cobbler, she can get you right back in tip-top shape! Ha. But in all seriousness, Tina had it going on! I admired the way she seemed to juggle all her responsibilities with such ease yet still found time to be a great friend, daughter, generous giver, and overall, great person. I took notes for when I would someday have a family of my own.

It wasn't until a few years into our friendship that she would share with me the details of what she had been through and how it shaped her life. I was shocked at first because the thought of experiencing the kind of trauma that she had was unimaginable. Then I was saddened and angry to know that my friend had gone through something so horrific. However, I was mostly amazed at her resilience, fortitude, and downright refusal to let the devil's attempt to destroy her life succeed. Her deep connection to God and her unwavering faith suddenly made sense. Only God could have brought her through something so painful, yet she remained unbroken. From the day I met Tina until now, she has always had the attitude that God's word is unfailing, His favor is unyielding, and His promises are true—*period*! If you try to argue this with her, I promise, that is an argument you will not win! I never understood why she was so convinced of God's faithfulness and why her stance was so unshakable until I learned of the battles she had walked through. Through it all, she leaned on God and refused to stay in the pit of despair and hopelessness. Like any soldier who has been in battle, she had some scars and wounds. But through the blood of Jesus and the healing power of His Word, she was restored and was able to overcome her adversity. She allowed God to turn her pain into purpose, her anger into an anthem of praise, and her bitterness into a blessing. Like the scripture says, "You have turned my mourning into joyful dancing. You have taken away my clothes of mourning, and clothed me with joy" (Ps. 30:11 NLT).

As you read this book, let it encourage you that no matter what difficulties you've been through or whatever traumatic situations you've faced, it does not have to be the end of your story! There is hope, joy, peace, and blessings waiting for you on the other side of despair! Let God speak to you and show you how to overcome as you read through these pages.

Jemia Ellis Wingard
Speaker, singer/songwriter, recording artist (Jemia)
Worship leader and teaching staff at Bridges Nashville church

Foreword

I was a freshman on the first day of high school, and I had gotten into a fistfight and subsequently suspended. The fight ensued because this sophomore told me that freshmen were not allowed to sit in this section of the mall (cafeteria) while slapping my sandwich out of my hand onto the ground while calling me derogatory names. Shockingly, this was also an African American female. That was also the first day I saw Tina! I was thirteen years old at Capistrano Valley High School in Mission Viejo, California. She was standing and dancing on the cement block in the mall around her senior friends and laughing and being joyful. Why not? She was a senior (as I would find out later after we met). How did I notice her? Well, besides her dancing and standing on a cement block, there were not many African Americans in 1990. So when you saw one, you were quite shocked. I have never seen so many African Americans at one school but granted this is now high school. Although we had only approximately twenty-five African Americans out of two hundred high school students, that was still a lot in 1990.

After returning to school from my three-day suspension, Tina made a point to find me at lunchtime and immediately walked over to me with that strong confident personality and presence about her. She asked me, "Why did you get into a fight the other day?" I told her what happened, and she responded, "You come sit with us seniors from now on!" Before long, she was taking me home from school or back to her house, going to Wednesday night Bible study together, and church on Sunday. Thirty years later, she's still a joyful person that doesn't let her emotions overrule her behavior no matter how big the struggle is. There are three words to describe Tina: bold, grounded, and tenacious! *Bold* in her God-given purpose, always *grounded* in the Word of God and continues to be a biblical teacher to me, and *tenacious* throughout her walk of life.

Proud to have her as my *big sister* and *role model!* Her book is going to change lives with her testimony!

Raquel McLaughlin
CEO/founder
Reimportation LLC
E-mail: info@ridesportation.com
Website: www.ridesportation.com

My name is Tina. I was born and raised in very strict Christian homes. Did you see the "s" on home? Well, that's what divorce will do. My parents divorced, and I was fortunate to grow up with both parents, still, just in two separate states. I was born in San Diego but eventually spent a lot of time with my mom's side in Tulsa / Broken Arrow, Oklahoma, and my dad's side in Corpus Christi, Texas. While I grew up an only child of theirs, I have two brothers and two sisters who later came after they were remarried with different spouses. My mom moved back to Oklahoma pursuing her music career, so I was able to spend an enormous amount of time with my cousins, aunts, uncles, and grandparents on the Pearson side. Then I'd spend the summers with my cousins, aunts, uncles, and grandparents on the Barnes side in Texas. My life was full of excitement because every year, summers and holidays were very different every time, depending on where I was and which part of my family I was around. The one constant, though, was the love and teachings of Christ that filled each home that left me no choice but to follow Jesus and his teachings. I grew up very confident in who I was yet very independent. My closest sibling in age was (and still is) nine years younger than me living in Texas. Therefore, growing up an "only child" is not a far stretch, and I naturally grew into a very self-confident young lady. Still to this day, I often receive compliments on the boldness I exude and how strong-willed of a person I present myself to be. That's why I'm writing this story. I grew up with so much love from my family and from the Word of God that the enemy (the devil or satan—he gets *no capital letters in my book*) tried everything to break me. I'm hoping that little girls and boys, even grown men and women, will hear and read this story to help get them over the edge. Yes, there were and are times when I get down and things don't go my (your) way. But I'm here to tell you that God is a faithful Father, and He loves His children. Now it's just a matter of *you* deciding if you're His child or not and if you're going to let Him be your Father. For me, I am His child, and while it seemed dark at the time of my horrific incident, I made it out, and I saw His hand in getting me out as well. I'm writing this story because at a confident point in my life, a very tragic event shook the confidence and independence right out of me. What you are about to read is my effort in sharing how I overcame one of the worst events that could happen to a person. Hopefully, you will receive hope and encouragement. Hopefully, you'll say that if Tina and God made it through that, then God and I will do the same through my horrific circumstance.

Taking You Back

My mother remarried. Now technically, the world would call the man that my mom and I lived with my stepfather. But I don't believe that. I believe if a man raises you, feeds you, clothes you, teaches you the things of God, then he is a father figure, spiritual father from God, and a nonbiological father. Therefore, I call him my father. All while I grew up, my mom was a nurturing, loving, and accepting person. Still to this day, I've never met anyone as open and nurturing as she was and is. She traveled a lot, pursuing her music career and was very, very good at it. At that time, she left me in very good hands. My father, who has his own miraculous story to tell, was and is a man that knew and walked with God.

He retired abruptly from the NFL, surviving a vicious poisoning and gave his life to Christ. He taught me the principles of Christianity, and he lived his life preaching and mentoring troubled youth via churches and prison ministries everywhere he went. He taught me and them about the goodness and blessings provided by the God he served. As a child, I would be awakened hearing him pray at four in the morning, and that's when I learned the habit and power of prayer. So being raised with and by him, I truly felt the covering and favor of God all around our dwelling and everywhere we went. Naively, I believed that nothing bad could ever happen to me because my life was just that great. I had God and I had my father, a six-foot-seven-inch, 320-pound former NFL defensive lineman Black man with a voice deeper that Barry White's, protecting me. I literally identified our God, the Father, with my father: a protector, provider, and a covering. I just knew I was well-protected from *all* hurt, harm, and danger. With all that I had,

1. my mom's natural prowess oozing within me,
2. the larger-than-life earthly father, and
3. the larger-than-him heavenly Father.

What could go ever wrong? My mom married him when I was three years old. From then to my late teens, I had everything that I needed and wanted. We were very blessed financially: we had money, we drove nice cars, and I was in the best of schools and neighborhoods. Now stop right there. I truly know that God is *more* than things, but remember, I was a kid: very visual, literal, and identified with what's seen. The "provision and protection" was very visible in my life back then. To a point, those visible things were, and still are today, an active belief I carry with God's presence working. The difference is that it was all about me then: *I* was the kid, and *I* was being blessed. Now those "things" are items given to me by God *to bless others* in which I come in contact. Nonetheless, my life was blessed and favored at every turn. I was popular at school with many friends, and I had a great social life. I had a life full of love, laughter, and peace. The two of them instilled a healthy fear (respect and reverence) for God. I learned that "character" meant that I should do the right thing even when no one was looking.

Fortunately, through the divorce, my mom knew that I loved my biological dad. She also had a decent-enough relationship with him, my daddy, as well. When I would travel in the summers to him in Texas, it was the same in all aspects. He was and still is a man that loved God and protected his family. Built with a strong work ethic, he was as disciplined as they come (i.e. drill sergeant status, LOL). I learned the value of order, discipline, and hard work. I believe it's from him that I naturally, of course, learned my entrepreneurial skills and leadership traits. I loved traveling there because I had so much fun with my cousins and brothers and sisters. It didn't hurt that my grandfather, Papa, would treat me like royalty too. So I felt loved everywhere I turned. On one hand, I had a pastor father in California, and on the other, I had a strict and disciplined daddy in Texas. On top of that, I had the rich Christian heritage of the both sides of grandparents.

If you hear nothing else, I need you to hear this: They *all* ran a tight ship, *and I mean tight*. I wasn't a perfect child but *almost* (I'm sure my cousins would say differently, but this is my book). I was the one that would come in at 10:58 p.m. on an 11:00 p.m. curfew. I would be one of the first ones in the house when the streetlight just began to flicker. The rule was, if you weren't in the house when the streetlights came on, it was time for a "whooping." I mean a serious whipping! My god! Just reminiscing about my cousins taking one of those openly violent, message-sending belt (or whatever was close) beat-down whippings makes me shiver. They were not having childish, devious moments from any of us. In a weird way, as I got older, I translated that respect for their authority into a true respect for the authority and power of God. Speed limits, school rules, or whatever, if it was a rule, law, or request from an adult, I was the first to obey. I'm so thankful that my parents believed in the Proverbs 13:24 verse:

> Whoever spares the rod hates their children,
> but the one who loves their children is careful to
> discipline them.

Well, they loved us, no doubt! My brother knew they loved him even as a fifteen or sixteen years old—my god! Oh, I pause just at the thought of that whoopin' I saw.

Some people would say it was strict while others would say it was too rigid. But for me, it was just my life. I knew nothing more and nothing less.

My mom, father, and I, at some point, moved to Laguna Niguel, California. There weren't many people that looked like me as far as my skin tone was concerned. However, in Texas, everyone looked like me, and life was perfect for me there too.

There again, I was only raised to believe we were all the same, so I didn't know any different. It really didn't matter where I went, every area including my neighborhood and my school, I found favor, and nothing bad ever happened around me.

Nothing Bad Could Happen to Me

(My Little Bubble)

At this point in my life, I had never seen anything tragic. I heard about it on television shows and even possibly through the news. However, I always saw things go my way, and I felt that the favor would follow me. Favor is a wonderful thing. We Christians say that it isn't fair because it's something that we do not deserve. Favor is truly a gift from God Himself. Ultimately, it's a belief of good things to happen and an actuality of things currently happening that perpetuate the belief of more blessings to come in every area of one's life. Favor is good things happening for you, opportunities opening for you, and people looking out for you all due to God's anointing and hand covering you in that area. For a basic example, let's look at a scenario of you getting a great parking space on a midmorning Black Friday shopping experience. Some would say that's great timing, but I and believers call that "opening of the parking spot" at that time of year, favor, whether it opens as soon as you get there or it's open on the row you turn down as others are circling frantically and recklessly. That "good thing" is called favor, God's favor on my life. That's as basic as it comes. The not-so-basic variety might show up when you watch the news later that evening and find out that a robbery occurred at 3:30 p.m. at a store on Fifth & Broadway. While you remembered being there today, your receipt says you were there at that exact same spot at 3:25 p.m. God's favor is not only keeping me away from that burglar at 3:25 p.m., but it's also keeping that person that was robbed at 3:30 alive and able to make it out of that situation. And even if you want to take it seventeen steps further, God's favor is allowing that rebellious robber to turn his life around in jail or somewhere else at some later point in his life when he realizes he could have been dead or in prison for an extended time after doing so many bad things.

So growing up how I grew up, I thought *and* believed, *nothing bad would ever happen to me.* Well, I was as *wrong* as *two left feet* on a unicorn bull.

Even today, there are countless people that don't "like me" as they look at me with preconceived notions. I've heard that they say that it seems like my life has *always* been perfect and that I have no problems. But I say glory be to God because while some of society's worst fears have happened to me, I'm thankful that I don't fit the look-like-it scenarios. Even more so, I'm blessed beyond my understanding because of those things. Because of the morals instilled in me from youth (i.e., do what's right because it's right, treat others how you want to be treated, etc.) the Christian values (God will protect you, His favor will sustain you, etc.), and the personal relationship with Christ (praying for direction, reading the Word of God to find out who I am and how to live, etc.), I found it easy and beneficial to make a habit of daily confessing the Word of God over my life. I began to develop a very strong sense of discernment due to the time I've spent in the Word of God. Over my younger years, I was taught by the Word of God and by my father to go where your favor was. If you go anywhere and the cloud (discernment of His presence) of godly favor is not there for you, then don't go or stay there. When the cloud moves, you move with it. I did exactly what God told me to do. If I did not believe God told me to leave, go, or stay, I didn't. Just like everyone else, I am a product of how I was raised, what I believe, the thoughts I think, and the decisions I make. I am so thankful to God for placing everyone in my life to help me see and believe.

My message to you is to believe. It doesn't matter what you're going through and what may come your way, believe. Believe what? Believe that the Word of God is true. Believe that God has a large part in your triumph over those things that seem insurmountable right now in the moment. Why? The answer to that question is simply because if you do not *actively and intentionally decide* to believe His word, your mind, accompanied with this problem, will cause you *not* to believe. Even when good things occur, you'll think it's "luck!" That's one word I absolutely hate! When you say "luck," it tells me that you believe that whatever good thing occurred is by happenstance. You just "so happened" to be in the right place, buy the right ticket, or do the right thing for that good thing to occur. "Luck" says that only you and your decision/timing had something to do with it and that N*o greater power, Holy Trinity, God as spirit, angel,* or *godsent person had anything to do with it.* Nonsense! Anyway!

*****

Year 1995
Fast-forward to my adult life

I made a trip to Nashville with my husband and my infant baby girl. We were helping a close family friend with an event. I enjoyed my time there, but it was not a place I wanted to move. You must remember that I lived a good portion on the beaches of California. So why on God's green earth would I ever *want* to move to Nashville? Well, God was up to something. While there, I heard the Holy Spirit tell me to pick up my things and move here. This city is going to be your new home, he said. The Holy Spirit then tells me, "I'm going to give you a business that you are going to run, helping men and women reclaim their lives. You will show them how to take care of and honor My temple, their bodies." So without a question, we moved! Please know that I was not excited about it. I'm a Cali girl, and I still wake up yearning for the beach. In Nashville, there wasn't a beach anywhere close, and *none* of the homes were stucco, ugh (LOL)! In obedience, I just moved with no questions asked. A short while later, the Holy Spirit led me on a three-day fast. On the fast, I was to read two books: *Who Moved My Cheese* by Dr.'s Spencer Johnson and Kenneth Blanchard and *I Wrote This Book on Purpose, So You May Find Out Yours* by John Stanko. At the end of the three-day fast, the

Holy Spirit dropped in my spirit, "Your Body His Temple." I didn't have a clue as to what this was or what this meant. Months passed before He thoroughly revealed to me that it was to be the name of my business. He explained that with it, I would train, educate, and lead by example, how to take care of His temple, our bodies. My first thought was, *Wrong*! I wanted to be a flight attendant, and he was going to bless that desire so, surely, he missed it. But even with my desire, I just obeyed His voice, especially with Him being the author and finisher. He won without a fight. As the insecurities began to sit in, feeling unqualified, unprepared, and having no experience, he led me to a school in Tennessee to get equipped to do my job. Lesson there: He provides for His will to be done in your life. After two babies, I started my journey as a certified personal trainer and nutritionist. I did it. I had *zero* clients, but I did it! I had no fears, though, because He said he would provide the people, and He did. There were a few more lessons I had to learn, though. Fortunately, I have been blessed to help countless men and women spiritually, mentally, and physically.

*****

Getting settled in Tennessee

Starting out, we stayed with the same husband-wife friends we helped on my initial trip until we got settled. My husband went to work every day, and we had one car with our baby girl. If I needed to get somewhere, I had several choices. I could wait on our friend, get up and get ready earlier than normal to take my husband to work, wait until he got off work, or wait until the car was free on the weekends. Remember, this all is happening in 1995–96 and well before Uber/Lyft.

Myself, son Tracey Jenkins, daughter Toni
Jenkins, and ex-husband Toney Jenkins

The Decision

So now that you know more about me and my background, you know that I'm a very disciplined person. Some would say anal. Not long after we established ourselves in Nashville, I had a few bills that needed to be paid. The due date was in two days, and I was adamant about paying them on time. I went through my choices. I asked my husband if he'd be able to take me to the mall to pay them. He was unsure because of his hectic work schedule and various meetings, so I asked our friends. Our friend mentioned that he may have been able to take me because he wasn't sure if he was going out of town for another event. Two (longggg) days have now passed, and the anal-punctual-adamant-Tina still had not locked in a ride to go pay my bills. I know what you're thinking. I could pay them online, right? Well, no. I just recently (twenty-five years later) became comfortable with online purchases and payments. Moreover, to this day, I still believe in the dying art of face-to-face true customer service. As you now know, I'm very strong in my beliefs. As strong as I believe in the Word of God, I must tell you that I do *not* believe in the five-day grace period that credit card companies give you, just as strongly. In my mind, that's just five more days they sit there and gouge you for more of your money with interest. I was not going to pay that money to them! At 6:00 a.m., the morning of the "due date," my father, the six-foot-seven pastor, calls me. In our conversation, he asks about my plans for the day. I told him I was somehow going to get to the mall today to pay some late bills, and that was the only thing that I had planned. He immediately said he felt in his spirit that I shouldn't go. What? Late bills? Oh no! Confident in my independence, young, and trying to be grown, I responded and said, "What's the big deal? It's just the mall. Besides, I have to go pay my bills!" He then says, "I just felt in my spirit you shouldn't go today. Maybe go tomorrow." Our conversation eventually ended, but I was bullheaded and strong-willed, so I still insisted on going. I just knew nothing would happen, to my core, I felt that everything would be fine, so I kept trying to find a ride. My husband said he would take me, but it wouldn't be until later that afternoon or evening. You should have seen my face. I didn't want to go later. I wanted to go during the day. A few hours later, my mother called. Unaware that my father had called earlier, she, too, asked what I was doing for the day. I told her the same thing, and as we talked, she said the Holy Spirit told her to tell me not to go to the mall that day as well. My face dropped. I couldn't believe that my parents were telling me to "pay my bills late," so I thought, *Were they playing a game? What?* I thought, *They didn't understand.* I was determined to go, though.

Hindsight being twenty-twenty, in my haste and in my flesh, I saw them as just my parents who had lost touch and didn't know anything. Unfortunately, that one and only time, I failed to see them as who they truly were in that moment. They were operating as my two most influential spiritual protectors under the guidance of the Holy Spirit. As you recall, I've never been rebellious, and I always listened to what they said, but I was so in tune with what I needed/wanted to do that I didn't listen. We, as believers, sometimes allow our flesh, our wants, and our desires to cloud our judgment, our ears, and actions. If you really meditate, pray, think about it with your spiritually renewed mind right now, there are things you should be doing right now and things you should stop doing right now. God has told you countless times and in, only God knows, how many countless ways the very thing you need to do. If this memoir does nothing else, I'll encourage you to follow God and His promptings. Of course, as a writer, I want you to keep reading and buy and share this book with as many people as possible. But right now, I am prompted by the Holy Spirit to ask you to stop reading (after this sentence), find a quiet space and place, and seek God on your next move, your next decision, and then come right back to this spot: *here*!

Okay, hello! Welcome back. I pray God's favor and anointing on whatever He told you or reminded you to do. I know it's going to be powerful for you and all those around you. Drop me a line (e-mail, tina@ybhtfitness.com or Twitter, @Trainer Tina or website, YBHTfitness.com) to let me know how God moved in that moment please.

Let's get back to it. As you recall, I was in my flesh, no different from you possibly just were before the pause, and I was just going to the mall to pay bills and come right back!

I didn't understand what the big deal was in my natural mind. I'm just going to the mall to pay bills; after all, I had to pay them on time, and today is the day. That's the anal, cut-and-dry, no-nonsense, black-and-white part in me. This was a time well before Uber and Lyft, and I wasn't very computer savvy, so paying online was not an option. I didn't trust that option anyway. So if you look at the big picture, I couldn't find a ride, both potential rides are up and down, my dad and mom had already fully warned me not to go. I not only went against the counsel of the two most important people in my life, but I was pressing against all natural means of transportation, and I still was so eager to go. Now that the entire day has gone, the friend who was up and down, finally called to say he was headed to the airport and that I could keep his car to get to the mall if I agreed to drop him off. "*Yes*, finally!" It is now way later than I originally planned on going, so I took him to the airport and went to the mall. I was finally glad to do what I wanted to do, needed to do: pay my bills today.

How My Life Changed Forever

With only an hour left, I strolled through the mall paying my credit card bills. I had seven total stops to make in an hour, so I was focused on getting them all paid. I never noticed someone following me. Walking through the mall, store to store, I paid my last bill and headed back to my friend's car. Please keep in mind, I was not very familiar with his car: which button did what, unlocking the car, or opening the door. That was very foreign to me. Well, I get to the car, open the door, and shut the door behind me. As I'm finding the correct key, I looked in the rearview mirror, and I see two guys bobbing, weaving, ducking, and hiding. It was from a distance, though, but they began to get closer and closer and closer. While scrambling and searching for the locks to lock the door, they snatched it open. The next thing I know, two guys were getting in the car! *Two*!

They said, 'Move over b———!'

At that moment, my heart sank! Scared out of my wits and my heart beating out my chest, I moved over. There was roughly $4,000 cash in my purse after cashing my husband's check, and my thoughts were everywhere. My first thought was for my baby girl, whom I love so dearly. She's just an infant. She needs me. I've got to get out of this. There were so many more thoughts: my mother, I'm her only girl; my dad, he's going to be devastated—he's six feet seven, and if he ever finds these guys, he will kill them; my husband, he's going to be filled with guilt that he didn't make it back in time to take me or make provisions to get me to the mall. The thoughts that go through your mind in these situations are endless, and they all happen at one time. What kept my mind, though, was the thought of my baby girl not having her mom. That one recurring thought was the one that made me say, "I'm getting out of here!"

Doing the only thing I knew to do, I said, "*The blood of Jesus!*" That "saying" goes back to the countless days and nights I saw and heard my father deal with different things growing up. I learned that the blood of Jesus healed and cured many ailments and situations. Well, I was in a situation, to say the least. In that car, there was a lot of switching back and forth on the front row. One of the guys wanted me to drive, so he switched me back to the driver's seat (remember, he first scooted me over when he got in). Then again, on second thought, he wanted me to drive. We literally switched again several times, and finally, we switched back, and he told me to start the car. Well, unbeknownst to all of us, one of those switches caused my pants to get stuck on the gear shift, which shifted the car out of park. I later came to know that all the back-and-forth movement pushed the gear shift down into neutral and the car would not start. Wait, did you see that in your mind? Was that favor? Let me explain. Question: How does an unstarted parked car shift to neutral? Answer: I have no *earthly* idea, but *spiritually*, I believe it was a movement of God. "Praise God, Hallelujah, thank you, Jesus" goes right there. God was working in that moment, but I'll come back to that! Now I'm in fear (and apparently, they were too) because I'm thinking, "Why isn't the car starting?" With the car not able to move, they decided that in that moment that they would rape me: right there in the mall parking lot!

Changed in an Instant

They felt there was nothing else to do, so they decided to change my life forever, change the innocence that I once had, change the mindset that I once had, change me from loving everyone to hating everyone, changed me from smiling all the time to crying violently through the day, change me from carefree living to looking over my shoulders, changed me from no medications to medications every day, changed me from upbeat to no beat in my step, whatsoever. My life was changed forever, but the biggest thing that changed was the newfound anger I had: *towards God.*

How could You let this happen to me? Why didn't You save me? Why didn't You protect me as your Word says You would? You sat there and watched me hurt, cry, scream for my life, and You never intervened. I didn't deserve this! I have lived my entire life for You. I told my friends about You. As far as I was concerned, I was going to raise my children to honor You, to tithe, to go to church, and to live a life of holiness. *Was this the repayment I got?* I was so dumbfounded. I was so lost. I was completely devastated.

The car *still* didn't start after they raped me. They were scared and started to panic. I later found out in court that they were out on "good behavior" from the detention center where they were detained, but they made plans to escape permanently and get back to Memphis. They told the judge that they planned on me driving them there where they would strangle me to death using my friend's guitar cord in the back seat and leave me on the side of the road.

But God! There was another plan that took effect: one, of which, I had no idea. They got afraid, jumped out the car, and left quickly with me still naked. I jumped out the car and headed back into the mall to get help. Half naked, I passed a group of people smoking and standing outside the entrance. Sadly, no one offered to help me. Not one! They had to have seen me distraught, disarrayed, and half naked, but no one offered a jacket, shirt, or anything for me to cover myself. I was completely at a loss for words. With no pants entering the mall, the first helpful and empathetic face I saw was a cop who immediately clothed me with his jacket. He covered me in his arms and told me everything was going to be okay. I cried in his arms and told him, "You have to catch them." He looked in my eyes and said, "I will catch them. You stay right here." I screamed with my biggest and loudest voice, full of tears. "They're in this mall. Please catch them!"

I sat there with head held low looking toward the ground, wondering if I was ever going to see my precious baby girl. I thought at that time I will never let this happen to her. All I wanted to do was hold her in my arms. As I looked up, there was one guy that asked me for my husband's address and phone number. He called to make him aware of what had happened, but to this day, we do not know the identity of that good man. What seemed like forever was only thirty minutes, but the cop came back, looked in my face, and told me that he captured both young men. That was good news, but I wanted an explanation, I wanted to know why, I wanted to know what made them look at my face and say, "I want to rape her." Why would they want to change my life forever? Why would they want to create devastation? I considered myself a very nice girl. I was not a promiscuous teenager having sex with everyone growing up. I was a virgin when I got married, and I still was a very nice girl with which to hang out. If anyone needed something, I would give it to them. Not my body of course, but just in general, I was a giver.

Now I was off to their mall security office to file a report.

This is the part that seemed like it took three days. I had to repeat what happened, had to describe what they looked like, and had to tell the officers specific details. That was the most horrifying thing ever. It almost was worse than the rape. Having to resay, repeat, and put into words the things that were done and the names that I was called was pure torture. Then, of course, they are now asking me how to get in touch with my parents. At that moment, trying to remember phone numbers was nearly impossible. I could not find my phone. I didn't remember anything. All I wanted at that moment was my baby girl and my dad to hold me, telling me everything was going to be okay.

Everything escaped me—my friend's number, their address in Antioch—my brain was not capable of retrieving those details. I had only lived there possibly two weeks before this happened. After dealing with the cop and going back and forth to my car trying to retrieve my cell phone, purse, and wallet, we finally narrowed down phone numbers and addresses. He called my father, and I'll never forget that call. I could hear the anger and the pain in his voice. The cop gave me the phone, and I confirmed what he said. Not even three minutes later, he was on the road to get his baby girl.

The crazy thing is, my father, the minister, worked in his passion going to different prisons to minister to young men that raped girls. My father had no desire for rape to hit his home, though. This event changed all our lives forever. Everyone put their lives on hold by moving in with me to take care of me. It was very difficult for me to function without prescription drugs and seeing a therapist sometimes up to four times a week. My day to day was pretty much sedated on prescriptions. The pain and memories were so real. As time went on, I began to slip into depression as I talked about it three to four times a week in "therapy." For me, though, the constant repetition was *not* making it any better, only worse. I was constantly rehearsing what happened. One day, a thought hit me while I was riding home from an appointment: "I don't want to do this anymore!" I was done with the drugs and the therapy rehearsals. I was listening to Donnie McClurkin's song "Stand," and I said to myself, "Lord, either you're going to be God in my life right now, or I'm going to be on these drugs for the rest of my life." I didn't have room for both! I poured the drugs out of my car, and I refused to go back to the therapist. From that day, I began to get stronger. I studied my Word, and I began to get strength. As I continued in my Word, I felt and believed the strength to take over the weakness. I eventually began to talk about it again, however, with a purpose this time. I wanted to help other young women that had been through the same thing. As strong as I had become, there was still something missing. As I moved forward, I realized that there was one thing that I hadn't done: *forgive them.*

Forgiveness

I remember reaching out to my lawyer, asking him for the address to the prison where they were placed. I remember to this day his face. He looked at me with his head tilted to the right side and said, "Why would you want that information?"

I replied, "I want to write them a letter."

"To curse them out?" he replied.

I laughed and said, "No, I want to write a letter to them to let them know that I've forgiven them."

Now with his head tilted to the other side and with a strange look on his face, he said, "Why would you want to do that?"

I responded, "*So that I can live.*"

See, what people fail to realize is that forgiveness is not for the one that wronged you—it's for you! It was for me, Tina! When you forgive, you can move on. I sent that letter, but I never heard back from them. I needed them to know that if they ever got out, I, nor my family, was not looking for revenge. I was not going to live my life with fear, bitterness, or anger. Truly, my intuition, awareness, and senses were heightened as I was forever changed in that capacity. I believe it has been a good change too. See, the devil will take what happens to you and mean it for harm, but God will take that very thing that happened and make it work for your good *and* for His glory. That's exactly what He did for me! I had to forgive my husband as well. After soul-searching, I realized that I was angry with him for never taking me to the mall as he stated that he would. I had to learn to walk in forgiveness daily with him.

The System

Court Dates

I had no idea that we were going to spend one to two years going back and forth in court with these young men and the detention center. To say unbelievably draining would be the understatement of the century. The most difficult day was watching them testify their intentions to take me to Memphis, use the electric guitar chord in the back seat to kill me, and then leave me on the side of the road. While it was extremely hard to hear, I soon realized that God was in the car with me! Angels of protection were in the car with me! The gear shifting out of park preventing the car from starting was a true act of the Holy Spirit. Act of the Holy Spirit? How can I say that? Well, I believe that He prevented the drive that led to their panic. He stopped the car from starting that led to their capture. Ultimately, He created a stall that prevented my death. I am so thankful! "Thank you, God!" Today I not only live a very prosperous and productive life, but I am also happy! I have no fear, and I'm not bitter. I'm not angry, and I received a gift in the chance to raise my daughter. I was blessed to have a beautiful son three years later, and he is, just like my daughter, my pride and joy! I am a firm believer that forgiveness is the key to a healthy and prosperous mindset! It's either God's way or no way for me! I recognize that God's presence and favor was with me as I grew up and especially there when the worst day of my life came.

I pray that my story has blessed you and helped you to see that you too can make it through. Life is real with tragedies. Terrible things happen to all of us, but despite all that we go through in this world, God's glory will be served as we go through it. That's what I mean when I say, "Go through it, God's way." The worst of worst things happened to me, but God saw to it that I would be able to help others by shining a light on things that would normally get lost in the tragedy. I'm so glad that He raised me in a family that helped to shape my vision. With a corrected vision, through and by the Word of God, we all can see His hand in things. For that I am grateful. If you take God's view, you are guaranteed to win as a child of His. "Winning" does *not* mean that horrible things will never happen. It just means that regardless to what happens, God's got your back, front, and both sides. It's just a matter of how you see it. Look at it like this, in that moment, I was a Christian and *all* the following happened to me: violation and protection, devastation and deliverance reckless behavior and life with purpose.

Scriptures That Got Me Through

Peace I leave with you; my peace I give you. I do not give to you as the world gives. Do not let your hearts be troubled and do not be afraid. (John 14:27)

Cast thy burden upon the Lord, and he shall sustain thee: he shall never suffer the righteous to be moved. But thou, O God, shalt bring them down into the pit of destruction: bloody and deceitful men shall not live out half their days; but I will trust in thee. (Ps. 55:22)

When I am afraid, I put my trust in you. In God, whose word I praise—in God I trust and am not afraid. What can mere mortals do to me? (Ps. 56:3)

He shall subdue the people under us, and the nations under our feet. (Ps. 47:3)

Be strong and courageous. Do not be afraid or terrified because of them, for the LORD your God goes with you; he will never leave you nor forsake. (Deut. 31:6)

Blessed are those who mourn, for they will be comforted. (Matt. 5:4)

We have suffered terror and pitfalls, ruin and destruction. Streams of tears flow from my eyes because my people are destroyed. (Lam. 3:47–48)

I called on your name, LORD, from the depths of the pit. You heard my plea: "Do not close your ears to my cry for relief." You came near when I called you, and you said, "Do not fear." You, Lord, took up my case; you redeemed my life. (Lam. 3:55–58)

About the Author

Tina is a boss lady with a heart of gold. She has the unique ability to love hard and be all in for most while possessing the discerning gift to forgive and walk away from others when necessary. She does this to protect and value the most important aspect of herself: her spirit. All her businesses and endeavors are to help others get a full grasp of taking responsibility to uplift one's mind, body, and spirit. In doing so, she protects hers with a veracity like no other.

Tina is certified in personal training and nutrition. We've heard so many of her clients and friends say that she is as real as real can get because she is a straight shooter. She's not one to mince words as her heart is for you to get better without excuses. Her true desire is for people to take health and fitness to their highest possible level. In doing so, she helps people to realize the importance of taking the food they eat seriously, recognizing the impact, negatively or positively, it has on your body. She'll help you dig deep to figure out what mental and spiritual triggers are causing you to, in one way or another, hurt yourself. That's just who she is.

She is a true woman of God with a little California sass and confidence. There are most that love her to no end, and as you can imagine, her husband and kids are a part of that group. Conversely, there are others not accustomed to such freedom and openness. It doesn't matter if you catch her at her studio, at a client's home, in the gym, or even at her own home, you are in for a treat because her personality will greet you with a warm, loving kindness that seems unbelievable to come from a face, form, and figure of a movie star. She's just that awesome in *every single way*!

Myself, daughter Toni Jenkins, son Tracey Jenkins, son Marcus B. Wilson, husband Marcus L. Wilson, and son Ryan Wilson

A huge Thank You to my Mom & Dad for stopping your personal lives & careers to take care of me after the rape as I was unable to take care of myself.

A huge Thank You to Kathy Troccoli for the continued support, flowers, and monetary gifts after the rape.

A huge Thank You to my silent investor for funding this endeavor, making the book happen, and believing in me.

I Thank You all.

CPSIA information can be obtained
at www.ICGtesting.com
Printed in the USA
LVHW020745021121
702225LV00012B/366